WHY EASTER?

Jesus Died for Us
So We Can Live Forever

STEVE DEACE

A POST HILL PRESS BOOK
ISBN: 979-8-88845-321-6

Why Easter?:
Jesus Died for Us So We Can Live Forever
© 2024 by Steve Deace
All Rights Reserved

Interior Design by Alana Mills

Post Hill Press
New York • Nashville
posthillpress.com

Published in the United States of America
1 2 3 4 5 6 7 8 9 10

For Amy, the best mother for my children

America is a special place to live. We are lucky to live in a free country where many people around the world wish they could live. But why is America so special?

America is special because it was founded on truths that God Himself brought into the world, and it is a place where we are allowed to celebrate those beliefs.

We can celebrate holidays like Easter because of how this country was created.

Easter is about more than just chocolate and bunnies. Easter is a celebration of God's greatest miracle, when Jesus died for our sins and was resurrected! But why did Jesus have to do that?

To understand why Easter is so important, we have to go back to the beginning, when God shared His rules for how we can live without sin.

These truths began with the Ten Commandments, which were God's first written words to us. He shared these Commandments through Moses, who was a follower of God even when it wasn't easy.

With God's help, Moses saved the people of Israel from slavery to rulers who were very mean to them.

Through Moses, God performed miracles that helped get His people to safety, like parting the Red Sea so the Israelites could walk on dry land to escape their enemies.

After His people traveled for many months, God called Moses to a very high mountain called Mount Sinai.

Now that God's people were free, they needed rules to show them how they should live peacefully.

He gave Moses the Ten Commandments, which were written in stone, so that they couldn't be erased. This way people knew how important it was to follow them.

These Ten Commandments are God's Law and help to show all of His Believers how we should live our lives, how to obey God, and how to know right from wrong.

Here are the
TEN COMMANDMENTS
in order:

1. God is the one true God. Anyone who says they are a god or says something else is a god is not telling the truth.

2. Don't make things and worship them as gods. It seems silly, but in the past some people would make pretend gods out of things like wood and pray to them. God wanted His People to know that they shouldn't do that anymore.

3. Don't use God's name as a bad word or make fun of it. It's important to respect God and show Him that we are thankful for all that He has done for us.

TEN COMMANDMENTS

4. Take a day of rest, like God did when He made the world, and use that day to worship God. You can even go to church!

5. Listen to your parents. God gave you parents to help teach you right from wrong and to keep you safe!

6. Don't kill. We should never harm another person unless we are protecting someone else's life.

7. Make sure you love your husband or your wife more than anyone except God, and make sure you treat them kindly.

TEN COMMANDMENTS

8. Don't steal from other people and take what doesn't belong to you.

9. Don't lie, especially to make yourself look better or to make someone else look bad. We shouldn't do bad things just because someone was bad to us.

10. Don't be jealous of what you don't have, but be thankful for what you do have. Everyone is different and has their own gifts and talents, and when we get jealous of other people, we might say and do things that hurt others.

God gave us these laws to make sure that we know how to live the best life dedicated to Him.

But if we don't follow His Laws, there could be consequences that we don't like.

Just like people today get in trouble for breaking the law, this is true of God's Laws too!

God wanted us to know that if we don't stop doing bad things, our separation from God could last forever!

Imagine being separated from the person you love most in the world, and how much you would miss them. It would be even harder to be separated from God.

See, God gave each of us a soul, which is the part of us that will live forever and ever.

After our body dies, our soul wants to go be with God where He lives in Heaven.

But He told us that no one who breaks His Commandments can be there, so that bad people and bad things can never get in.

That's why when we break God's Commandments, we risk not getting to be with God forever!

And as much as we'd be sad about not being with God forever, He would be even sadder not being with us, because He's the one that made us, and no one loves us more than God.

God literally counted every hair on your head. He knows your name. He hears your prayers.

The sad thing is, there is something inside of us that makes us want to do bad stuff sometimes. This is what God calls sin.

Sometimes we don't even want to do bad stuff, but we can't always stop ourselves, and we end up breaking God's Laws.

This is why sometimes we can be so mean to our parents or our best friends, people we love a lot.

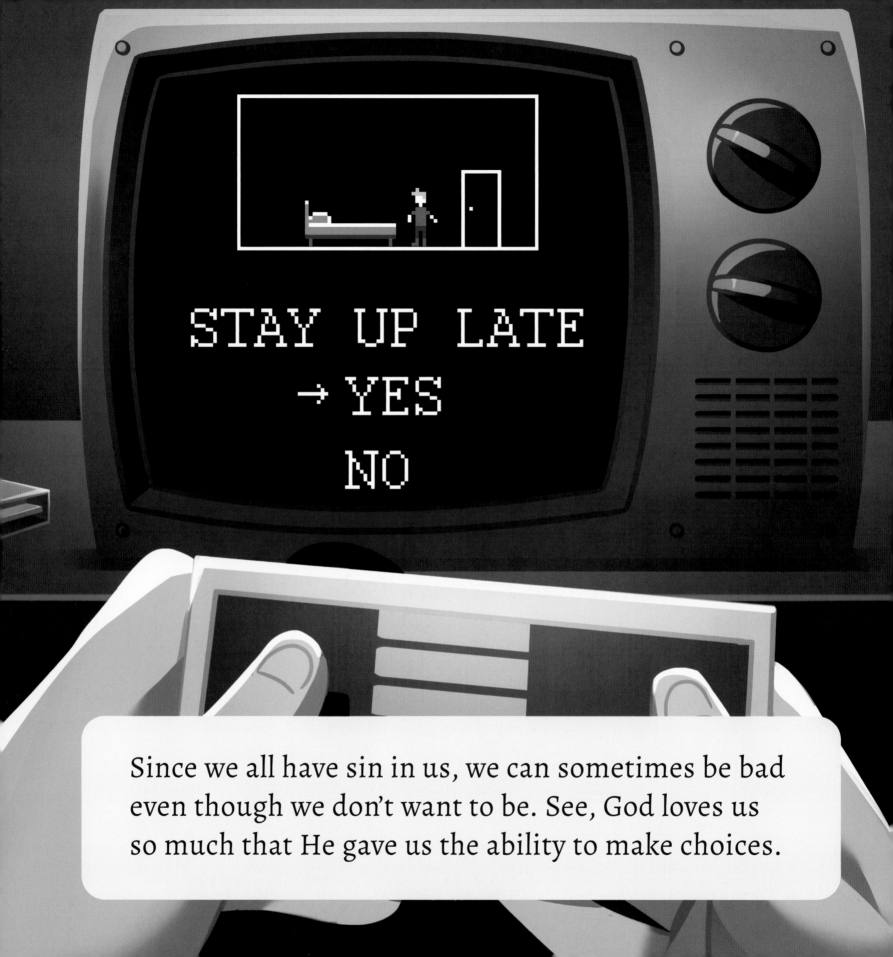

STAY UP LATE

→ YES

NO

Since we all have sin in us, we can sometimes be bad even though we don't want to be. See, God loves us so much that He gave us the ability to make choices.

He didn't make us to be like players in a video game that He controls by pushing buttons.

He gave us the freedom to make our own choices and showed us His love by telling us the right choices to be made.

We show God we love Him by obeying His Commandments, so when we disobey Him, we are really saying that we don't love Him and that we love things that are bad for us more.

But what does sin have to do with Easter? See, God also knows that sometimes we can't stop disobeying Him, even if we really want to do the right thing.

And He knew we needed His help! That's why God came to us in the form of a child, and His name was Jesus.

This is the Christmas story you may know, starting with the little baby born in the manger that would grow up to become a mighty savior for us all!

But first, Jesus chose to live like we do and face the same problems we do. Because while He was fully God, He was also fully human like us, and He wanted to show us that He understood everything we go through.

That's why Jesus had to have His diaper changed as a baby, just like you.

He had to be potty trained, and learn how to walk, talk, and read, just like you. He had to get a job to pay for His food and home as an adult, just as you will one day.

And that's why He learned from His earthly dad, Joseph, how to build things with His own hands.

While He grew up, Jesus lived a perfect life, free of sin. And finally, once He was old enough, He announced Himself to the world.

He started to share the good news that God had made a way to save us from sin and talk about the miracles of God.

He healed the sick, cured the blind, and made only a few fish and two loaves of bread into a giant feast! He taught that since we couldn't get to Heaven because of the bad stuff we'd done, that Heaven had come to us.

He taught us that in order to stop disobeying God, we need to tell God we are sorry and ask Him to give us the power to do what is right.

The people were listening to Him sharing the truth. They saw His miracles and started to believe.

But there were some people who did not want to listen or believe. These people did not like that Jesus was saying He was God.

And they really didn't want to hear that they needed to tell God they were sorry. So, after a while, they arrested Jesus.

They beat Him very badly, and then put Him to death on what is called a cross, which is a very painful way to die.

And even when they were hurting Jesus, He didn't get mad at those who did this to Him, but instead He prayed for them to be forgiven.

This was His way of showing God's love, and helps us to know that He is willing to forgive us for anything bad we may have done, too.

After He had died, they put Him in a tomb, which was a cave with a giant rock to cover the opening. But three days later, on the day we call Easter, the most incredible thing to ever happen took place!

God rolled away the giant stone that covered the tomb, and Jesus was alive again, proving once and for all that He really was God with us.

Because no one but God would have the power to come back from death.

By coming back from the dead, Jesus showed us that all of His teachings were true and we could trust Him with all things.

He died for our sins, so that we could be forgiven and go to Heaven. Jesus has promised to return some day and defeat all the evil in the world.

Before He returned to Heaven, Jesus gave us His Spirit, to help guide us away from sin and bring us to salvation.

If we ask God to forgive us and thank Him for raising Jesus back to life, Jesus will come and live inside of us.

This way, we can be with God all the time, even before we get to Heaven!

This is why we celebrate Easter, to thank God for sending Jesus to die for our sins and save us. And we are lucky to live in a country where we can celebrate Easter and God's love freely!

That wasn't always the case. When our country was first started, we were still under the control of a mean king, who wanted to be the only one that people worshipped.

Our Founding Fathers knew that they needed to fight for our freedoms so that they could believe in God and not be controlled by the king.

Since Jesus now lived inside of them, they wanted to follow God's Commandments and live by them. The Founding Fathers called this liberty, and they were willing to stand up for it.

And they did! God heard their prayers and eventually our Founding Fathers won their freedom and created a new nation—the United States.

One of the first things they did was make sure people had the right to go to church, read the Bible, and talk about God whenever they wanted to.

Because they knew without all those things, it wouldn't be possible for a special place like America to happen.

Now we are free to celebrate our love for God whenever we want, learn about Easter and the Ten Commandments, and welcome Jesus into our hearts, just as the Founding Fathers did.

And now you know why Easter is God's greatest miracle. For God loved us so much, that He gave us His Only Son, Jesus, to pay the penalty for our sins and mistakes that we couldn't pay ourselves.

HE IS RISEN

And if we truly believe that, with all our heart, then Jesus will come to live in our hearts now and we will live with Jesus forever in Heaven. Even after our body dies. This is why God sent His son to our world—to save our world.